Behold the Gift ...

the Blessings of Bethlehem

thoughts by Karen Anderson
painting by Kathie Hanson

His Good News
was difficult to comprehend ...

so God made it beautifully simple ...

a baby ...

from God's Word ...

And she gave birth to her firstborn, a son. She wrapped him in cloths and placed him in a manger, because there was no room for them in the inn.

And there were shepherds living out in the fields nearby, keeping watch over their flocks at night.

An angel of the Lord appeared to them, and the glory of the Lord shone around them, and they were terrified.

But the angel said to them, "Do not be afraid. I bring you good news of great joy that will be for all the people. Today in the town of David a Savior has been born to you; he is Christ the Lord. This will be a sign to you; you will find a baby wrapped in cloths and lying in a manger."

Suddenly a great company of the heavenly host appeared with the angel, praising God and saying, "Glory to God in the highest, and on earth peace to men on whom his favor rests."

When the angels had left them and gone into heaven, the shepherds said to one another, "Let's go to Bethlehem and see this thing that has happened, which the Lord has told us about."

Luke 2:7-14

come ... experience the Gift ...

for

the glory of God ...

"Behold the Gift ... the Blessings of Bethlehem"
by Karen Anderson

Moments Publishing
5315B FM 1960 West #152
Houston, Texas 77069
281-989-3812
fax: 281-379-2002
orders: www.MomentsPublishing.com
e-mail: info@MomentsPublishing.com

Copyright © 2008 by Karen Anderson
Printed in the United States of America

Edition ISBN: 0-9818896-4-6

Scripture taken from the HOLY BIBLE,
NEW INTERNATIONAL VERSION ®

© 1973, 1978, 1984 by International Bible Society.
Used by permission of Zondervan. All rights reserved.

Cataloging Data:
Anderson, Karen
Behold the Gift ... the Blessings of Bethlehem
ISBN-13: 978-0-9818896-4-1
1. Religious   2. Christmas   3. Jesus Christ
4. Devotional 5. Gift Books 6. Poetry

In honor of
my mother, Beverly Malick Kennedy,
and in memory of
my father, Ken Malick,
who first lovingly told me about
the Blessings of Bethlehem ...

In thanksgiving for
my family who gives honor to Him
by sharing that Good News ...
Ernie Anderson and Ryan Anderson
Eric, Kristin, Adeline, Julia and Lily Claire Hill
Paul, Melanie, Rhodes and Anderson Jackson

In gratefulness to my sisters ...
Kathie Hanson
for her faithful support and for the
beautiful painting of Mary and the infant Jesus ...
and Bobbie Preston
for her endless encouragement ...

With joy for
Howard Kennedy who loves us all ...

May you each be continually surrounded by
the Blessings of Bethlehem ...

with my love ...

Prepare my heart, oh Lord,
for the Blessings of Bethlehem ...
help me to be ready, once again ...
let me be in awe
of a singing sky
ushering in the majesty of God
through the humility of a child ...

let me be astounded
by the humble story of glory
nestled in a hard wooden bed ...

let me pause as
the very pulse of the universe
is gently heard in an infant's sigh ...

open my eyes
with renewed joy
and thanksgiving
and reverence ...

join me, Lord, I pray,
in the journey toward that Bethlehem manger ...

grant me, Lord,
a convicted and committed heart ...

let me feel the holy ground beneath my feet ...
let me bow at eternity's Gift ...
let me gaze upon the infant Son of God
who slipped in through that stable door ...

in the holy name of Jesus, I pray ...
Amen

THE JOURNEY ...

One

<u>AN ORDINARY DAY</u>

It was just an ordinary day ...

no parade ...
no fireworks ...
business as usual ...

but that ordinary day
changed the heartbeat of the world forever ...

for on that ordinary day
heaven came down to earth ...

and the Word became flesh ...
and the Word became real ...
and the Word dwelt among us ...

for on that ordinary day
a dirty stable became holy ground ...
a small infant slept beside the creatures
that He himself had created ...

for on that ordinary day
the skies ushered in a great star ...
shepherds came to kneel
before the Great Shepherd ...
and jeweled and crowned men
worshipped
the Crown of Crowns ...

for on that ordinary day
angels sang and hope was born ...

a tiny child became
the Prince of Peace ...
and
the King of Kings ...

for me ...
for you ...
for all people
everywhere ...

for on that ordinary day
God's love
became
touchable
and eternal ...

for on that ordinary day
a tiny babe came
not to live
but to die ...

and a tiny cradle
led to a cross ...

so that no day would ever be
ordinary again ...

TWO

<u>DECORATING</u>

It is time to decorate, Lord ...
please help me
so that I do it
in honor of You ...

I have lots and lots of boxes and bows ...
but I want to place the important things first ...

I want Your light to brighten my windows ...
I want Your peace to lay at each doorstep ...
I want Your love to fill each room ...
I want Your hope to grace each nook ...
I want Your joy to linger in my halls ...

I want to remember
that it is not "what" is
under the tree
that matters ...

I want to remember
that "who died"
on the tree
is what matters ...

come, Lord ...
help me decorate ...
for You ...

Three

THE CHRISTMAS WHISPER

The Christmas whisper ...
"He is here ... He is here" ...

the Christmas whisper began
long, long ago ...

as a Bethlehem stable became a holy place
and the awaited Messiah was born ...

even as the new and tiny King
breathed His first breaths,
believing people began to rejoice
and to give thanks
and to share
the Christmas whisper ...
"He is here ... He is here" ...

two thousand years later
people continue to fall to their knees
in worship and thanksgiving ...
"He is here"
"He is still here"
"He is right here"
"He is ever here"

so the whisper goes on ...
and it can be heard
among families ... among friends ...

among total strangers
reaching out to each other ...

it can be heard
when we work ...
when we play ...
when we worship ...
when we love ...
when we wonder ...
when we seek ...
when we pray ...

it can be heard
during our brightest moments
or on our darkest days ...

during times of building up
or in times of mending ...

and in just the everyday beauty
and miracle moments of life ...

yes, the blessed Christmas whisper continues,
and its truth has never changed ...

listen ...
hear with your heart ...
"He is here"
"He is still here"
"He is right here"
"He is ever here"

Joy to the World!

Four

STABLE VISITORS

I want to be a stable visitor ...

like the angels
appearing from nowhere ...
content to be nameless ...
whose very presence radiated His presence ...
whose voices sing of the manger miracle ...

like the shepherds
walking under the star of Bethlehem ...
guiding ...
directing ...
caring when even one is lost or hurt ...

like the wise men
acting upon God's Word ...
caring not about the length
or the cost of the journey ...
offering priceless gifts
in honor of the true King ...

stable visitors ...
those who intentionally
tread holy ground ...
those who know that
the love wrapped in swaddling cloths
was meant to be shared ...
those who know that Christmas began when
the Word became flesh ...

those who understand
that Christmas would continue when
the Word lived in our flesh ...

Lord, help me to know ...
that I need not travel to Bethlehem
to be part of Your nativity ...

prod me ...
teach me ...
to be a stable visitor ...

celebrating that cradle
turned throne ...

for if I did that each day
in your honor,
Bethlehem could be here ...
and now ...

and then
every day
could be
Christmas ...

Five

HOW COULD IT BE

How could it be
that a helpless babe lying in a manger
would one day
become the strength of our world ...

how could it be
that a soul so tiny
would one day
guide kings and peoples of all nations ...

how could it be
that feet two inches long
would one day
cross over the boundaries of hatred and prejudice ...

how could it be
that a faint whisper of a voice
would one day
be heard around the world ...

how could it be
that tiny, little shoulders
would one day
hold the weight of the world ...

how could it be
that those squinting eyes
would one day
see past the limits of earthly wisdom ...

how could it be
that a heart tucked into a chest so small
could hold all the love of the world ...

how could it be
that an infant cradled in a stable
could be the very One
who created
everything surrounding Him ...

how could it be
that the tiny, swaddled arms
would one day
stretch wide and willingly
upon a cross ...

how could it be
that the tiny hands
once held by wise men and shepherds
would one day
bear nail scars for each of us ...

how could it be, Lord,
that Your heavens
could knowingly declare ...
that someone as unlikely as a fragile infant
would one day
be our promise for tomorrow ...

how could it be, Lord ...
that You loved us so much
that unto us
this child was born ...

Six

THE MASTER'S PLAN

The Master's plan ...
Christ in a cradle ...

and hope was born ...
and peace was born ...
and love was born ...

the gift of hope that refreshes and rebuilds ...
the gift of hope that redeems ...

the gift of peace as we sit in His presence ...
the gift of peace provided by His power ...

the gift of love undeserved ...
the gift of love unconditional ...

the Master's plan ... Christ on a cross ...
and hope, peace and love were resurrected ...
and hope, peace and love became eternal ...

the Master's plan ...
so that the joy of His hope, peace and love
would always be mine ...
and would always be yours ...

Rejoice! Receive!
It is the Master's plan ...

Believe the plan! Live the Gift!

Seven

BEHOLD THE GIFT

A singing sky
boldly introduced the majesty of God ...
Behold ... the Story ...

through the tender gentleness of an infant child ...
Behold ... the Miracle ...

and eternal glory lay snug in a manger bed ...
Behold ... the Son ...

the hope of the world heard in a baby's tiny sigh ...
Behold ... the Promise ...

who came to live and to love among us ...
Behold ... the Prince of Peace ...

walking among us then and who does still ...
Behold ... the Messiah ...

the King who needed not an earthly throne ...
Behold ... the Savior ...

The Babe of Bethlehem ...
The Only Begotten Son ...
The Alpha and The Omega ...

Behold the Gift ...

Eight

SOUNDS OF THE HOLIDAY

Shhh ... listen ...
can you hear
sounds of the holiday?

honking horns, clinking coins ...
parades, parties, pageants ...
laughing elves and Santa's ho-ho-ho ...
jostling gifts, jingling bells,
trumpets, tubas and talking toys ...
handbells, hand claps and candlelight carols ...

shhh ... listen ...
can you imagine
sounds of that holy Bethlehem day?

a baby sighing ...
a mother humming ...
animals rustling ...
shepherds exclaiming ...
angels proclaiming ...

Lord, quiet my heart ...
help me to imagine ...
help me to absorb
the meaning of
the sounds born
in that stable sanctuary ...

and then today ...
may the sounds from my lips linger on ...

words of love
and grace ...

whispers of hope
and healing ...

songs of joy
and thanksgiving ...

prayers of praise
and peace ...

may these sounds
be a joyful noise to You,
my Lord ...

Happy holiday, Lord ...

Happy birth day, Lord ...

Happy holy day, Lord ...

Nine

I STAND IN AWE

We have heard of a baby
growing up to become a king ...
but only once
have we heard
of a King becoming a baby ...

I stand in awe of the story ...
the simple becoming sacred ...

I stand in awe
that a virgin, teen girl trusted God ...

I stand in awe
that a stable became a sanctuary ...

I stand in awe
that God wrapped something so wonderful
in a baby blanket ...

I stand in awe
that a shining star
pierced the sky with a blaze of glory ...

I stand in awe
that the quiet birth
was proclaimed by
clusters of singing angels ...

I stand in awe that wise men
still fall to their knees in His presence ...

I stand in awe
that hearts can be brought
from panic to peace
with just the whisper of His name ...

I stand in awe
that He is my Light ... my Anchor ...
my Hope ... my Joy ... my Peace ...
my model of pure Love ...

I stand in awe
that His birth was God's gift to me ...

I stand in awe
that He came not because I deserved it
but because I did not ...

I stand in awe
that He came not to live ... but to die
so that I could live and never die ...

I stand in awe of the story ...
cradle to cross ...
manger to Messiah ...

two thousand years ago
God sought to change the world
with just a humble servant ...

He still does so today ...

Ten

GIFTS OF HIS MOMENTS

Today, I sat beneath the tree counting my gifts ...
oh ... not the ones wrapped in pretty paper,
but the ones tucked within my heart ...
gifts from Him ... gifts of His "moments" ...

moments of love
when I feel His presence ...
moments of darkness
when I feel His promises ...

moments of wonder
when I stand in awe ...
moments of laughter
when I feel His pleasure ...

moments of tenderness
when I feel His touch ...
moments of joy
when I feel His pulse ...

moments of service
when I see His hand ...
moments of brotherhood
when I see no boundaries ...

moments of change
when I see Him as the constant ...
moments of calm
when He whispers His peace ...

moments of awareness
when I see past myself ...
moments of another's caring
when I see His face ...

moments of bounty
when I am humbled by my blessings ...
moments of trial
when I get to lean on Him ...

moments of despair
when He carries me ...
moments of glee
when He dances with me ...

moments of grace
when I am showered so abundantly ...
moments of mercy
when I so humbly receive ...

moments of forgiveness
when I seek to try again ...
moments of family and friendship
when I feel His connectedness ...

and for the greatest moments of all ...

Bethlehem ... the moment He came ...
and Calvary ... the moment He promised to stay ...

moments ... holy moments ...
Messiah moments ...
for these gifts I give thanks ...

Eleven

<u>MARY ... GOD'S SERVANT</u>

Mary was a humble servant of God ...
anointed with His miracle ...

and Mary just believed
because Mary's heart knew ...

He plans for His children ...
He provides for His children ...
He protects His children ...
He guides His children ...

Mary just knew
God has His plan ...
and His purposes
could include
even her ...

Mary used
the humbleness of her soul
to raise up
the majesty of Him
who formed her ...

Mary used
her simple life
to lift up the life
of the One who would be
her Son ...
and her Savior ...

Lord, I want to be like Mary ...

simply believing ...
simply obeying ...
passionately loving You ...
exalting You ...
living for You ...
doing for You ...
I want to say "YES" to You ...

I want my story
to be Your story ...

my Lord, I pray ...
use my humble brokenness
to mend walls for You ...

use my stumbling life
to bring others to Your light ...

use my stammering words
to speak boldly in Your name ...
this I pray, my Lord ...
for You can use
all of Your people
for Your purposes ...

nothing is impossible for You ...

You have done
great things for me, my Lord ...
may I, even I ...
step out to do great things for You ...

Twelve

THE STORY

The story
began
in
the beginning ...
and generations
upon generations
have added their chapters ...

one piece of the story took place in a stable ...

and continued in a carpenter's shop ...

and on a hillside in Nazareth ...

and on a fishing boat ...

and at the feet of small children ...

the story continued
on a donkey in Jerusalem ...

in a garden at Gethsemane ...

then on a cross at Calvary ...

it was the Good News ...
it was the best news ...

and the story still continues ...

in quiet moments and gentle whispers ...
in loud hurrahs and joyful hallelujahs ...
in grand places of worship ...
in the tiny crevices of private hearts ...

and the story continues each time
one kind word lifts another ...
one simple gesture buoys a soul ...
one promise of peace takes down walls ...
one shunned soul is made a brother ...
one broken soul is handed hope ...
one searching heart is offered the answer ...

and the story
lives on
and on
and on
each time we say "YES"
to the story ...

THE story of all stories ...

may we read it ...
may we believe it ...
may we live it ...
may we share it ...

Thirteen

HE IS HERE

The babe of Bethlehem
became the Christ of the cross ...

and those who sent Him there
sent Him to the tomb ...

and later there were those who cried,
"He is not there" ...

No ... He is NOT there ...
He is HERE!

He is in the morning dew ...
and in the evening stars ...

He is in every cell ...
and on every mountain top ...

He is in every cry ...
and in every sound of joy ...

He is in every act of kindness ...
and in every display of love ...

He blows through the soul ...
and through the wind ...

His name is whispered by children
and by old men ...

He is in every minute ...
and in every hour ...

He is here for you ...
and He is here for me ...
tomorrow and the day after ...
and for all times ...

so, then ...
what do we say to those who still cry,
"He is gone" ...

to them we say ...
"put on eyes of believing and
look past the cross ...
look past the tomb ...
look to the moments of your life ...
look around for He IS here!
He is right here!"

yes ...
their shouting took Him to the cross
and to the tomb ...

yes ...
their shouting took Him there ...

but our looking ...
our believing ...
our shouting ...
keeps Him HERE ...

Fourteen

HANDS

Tiny, pink hands of a babe in a manger ...
and there were those
who knelt in worship ...

strong, growing hands of a young carpenter ...
and there were those
who listened in awe at His wisdom ...

caring, compassionate hands
of the One who performed miracles ...
and there were those
who praised Him in thanksgiving ...

waving, sure hands
of the King arriving on a donkey in Jerusalem ...
and there were those
who cheered ...

determined, prayerful hands in the garden ...
and there were those
who ached as He was betrayed ...

beaten, thorn-scratched hands carrying the cross ...
and there were those
whose hearts were breaking ...

bleeding, nail-scarred hands
on the cross of Calvary ...
and there were those who wept ...

outstretched, comforting hands of the risen Lord ...
and there were those
who rejoiced ...

I pray that my hands
will forever
lift in praise to Him ...

I pray that my hands
might reach out to others ...
and that my touch
might lead someone else
to know His touch ...

I pray that my hands
might serve the One
who holds me
in His hands ...

the very hands that crafted the manger ...

the very hands that crafted the cross ...

for me ...

Fifteen

LOVE CAME AT CHRISTMAS

No room in the inn
so a stable became holy ground ...

love came at Christmas
wrapped in the skin of a baby Messiah ...

what gifts could I bring to His throne ...

what gifts could I offer that might honor Him ...

perhaps I could just ...

love greatly

give freely

walk determinedly

speak gently

respect openly

ask believingly

wait patiently

look expectedly

perhaps I could just ...

praise gratefully

proclaim joyfully

honor grandly

witness boldly

serve humbly

perhaps I could just
seek to be
an imitator of Him
and His ways ...

by being
His hands ...
His heart ...
His mind ...
His mouth ...
His feet ...
for His purposes
on this earth ...

perhaps I could just
do that this day ...

and the day after ...

and the day after ...
for Him ...

Sixteen

COME TO THE MANGER

How amazing that a Gift so great
would be so small ...

come to the manger ...
absorb the enormity of the present ...
a tiny baby
in swaddling cloths ...

an infant who will be called
Abba, Advocate, Almighty ...
the Alpha and Omega ...
who will be the Anchor, the Answer ...
the Anointed One ...
who will be called the Bread of Life ...
the Christ ... the Cornerstone ...
Wonderful Counselor, the Creator ...
to be named the Eternal, the Everlasting ...
the Exalted One ... Emmanuel ...
who will be held as our Example ...
and will be our Father, Friend, our Foundation ...
the Good Shepherd ...
the Healer, the Holy Spirit, the High Priest ...
to be called Immortal, Jehovah ...
the Lamb ... our Lord ...
He will be the Master, Majesty,
and the Most High ...
Mighty God ... the Messiah ...

He will be Omnipotent, the Prophet, the Potter,
the Prince of Peace ...

the Risen One, Restorer, our Refuge ...
our Rock and Redeemer ...
hearts will know Him as Sovereign, Savior,
and Teacher ...
He will be the Victor, the Vine, the Virgin's Son ...
praised as the Word and the Way ...

yes, the Gift there in the manger is Jesus ...
the name above all names ...
hallowed be His name ...

come to the manger and embrace Him ...
kneel with the undeserving crowd who gathers ...
together we will become known as
His Ambassadors, His Believers, His Beloved ...
His Branches ...
the Children of God, the Cloud of Witnesses ...
His Disciples, the Faithful, His Followers ...
the Forgiven ...
the Holy Nation, Living Stones ...
the Royal Priesthood ...
the Redeemed, Salt and Light ...
His Servants ...
all called to be His Imitators ...

the small baby
who came to get nothing but to give everything
calls us to the manger ...

and He calls us by name ... come ...

Seventeen

<u>GIVING GIFTS</u>

Heavenly Father ...
this is a busy season ...
a season of gift giving ...
it is a time
when we celebrate the greatest gift ...
the Gift of Your Son ...

Lord, this year
I would like to give precious gifts ...

I ask that You please guide me ...
in wrapping up handfuls of hope
for those who need to witness Your light ...

lead me, I pray ...
in presenting packages of peace
to those whose hearts and times are turbulent ...

encourage me, Father ...
in gathering baskets of joy
for those whose lives are dim ...

prod me in offering, precious Lord ...
bushels of love
to those who ache for Your touch ...

perhaps, Holy Father ...
You could help me to deliver these gifts
anonymously ...

so that the only gift card
would
bear
Your
name ...

these things
I want to do
in Your Son's honor ...

for
His birthday ...

no matter
the date
or the
time of year ...

I just want
to close my eyes
each evening and
whisper ...

I did that for You, Jesus ...

Happy
Birthday!

Eighteen

NO ROOM IN THE INN

No room in the inn ...
that's what they said ...

that's what I sometimes say now ...

I say ...
I am really busy today, Lord ...
today, Lord, I am rushed ...
but tomorrow ...
tomorrow would be a great day
to greet You ...
to spend time with You ...
to worship You ... to serve You ...
tomorrow I will come to the manger ...
tomorrow I will sit at the foot of the cross ...
yes, tomorrow would be a great day ...

and You just wait for me ...
no matter how long it takes ...

Lord, help me to empty my heart's "inn" today ...
help me to fill every corner with You today ...

Help me to say ... "today,
there is NO room in my heart
that is NOT of YOU" ...

come in, my Lord ...
fill all my heart's spaces with You ...

Nineteen

FEAR NOT

The angels proclaimed,
"Fear not" ...

and because of that infant King,
we can
"Fear not" ...

we can replace
the fear of despair
with His hope ...

we can replace
the fear of loneliness
with His presence ...

we can replace
the fear of sadness
with the joy of His Spirit ...

we can replace
the fear of daily wars
with His peace ...

the manger was filled to fill me ...
the cross was emptied to free me ...

so that I can believe
and say,
"Fear not" ...

Twenty

<u>KNOWING PEACE</u>

Today, I whispered a prayer
that our world may know peace ...

the peace that would awaken us in the morning
and walk with us throughout the day ...

the peace of love
that could softly encircle our world ...

the peace of brotherhood
that believes we are of one family ...

the peace of caring
that ushers in gentleness and warm friendships ...

the peace of laughter
that welcomes smiles and releases tensions ...

the peace of knowing
that surrounds true wisdom ...

the peace of awareness
that keeps our consciousness alive ...

the peace of kindness
that allows us to soften hurts and heal wounds ...

the peace of hope
that confirms that there is a reason to pray ...

the peace of gratefulness
that brings us humbly to our knees ...

the peace of understanding
that comes from risking ...

the peace of resolution
that comes from facing problems ...

the peace of commitment
that takes us closer to our vision ...

the peace of God's Good News
that could guide the hearts of all ...

the peace of our Lord
born that day in Bethlehem ...

the peace that stretches past time ...

past boundaries ...

past the differences of race ...

Christ's peace for this world ...

that could begin with me ...

and with you ...

each morning as we wake ...

Twenty-One

<u>A GOD LIKE YOU</u>

Who is a God like You?

I cry out ...
You answer ...

I hurt ...
You have compassion ...

I stumble ...
You walk beside me ...

Who is a God like You?

I sleep ...
You wake the dawn ...

I grow stale in my wonder ...
You call the waves to shore ...

I seek beauty ...
You raise up the tulips ...

Who is a God like You?

I am confused ...
You clarify ...

I judge ...
You love ...

I sin ...
You forgive ...

Who is a God like You?

I see a manger holding a baby ...
You deliver a King
holding my future ...

oh, my God,
how humbly I bow down ...

before Your faithfulness ...
before Your grace ...
before Your mercy ...
before Your majesty ...
before Your mighty plan ...

Who is a God like You?

I whisper my prayers ...

and You,
the
King
of
Kings,
hear my heart ...

I bow down ...

oh, my Lord,
I bow down ...

Twenty-Two

<u>SEEING GOD</u>

Our hearts can see God
in an infant Messiah
swaddled in the hopes of the world ...

in the singing angels
and the trumpeting sky
that announced His birth ...

in the Son of God
as He walked the earth ...

in the Lamb of God
who carried our burdens
to a rugged cross ...

our hearts can see God
in the comfort and peace
of believers who whisper His name ...

in those who stand united
by falling on their knees ...

in strangers and neighbors
who comfort, counsel and serve ...

our hearts can see God
as He gives Himself to those who ask ...

our hearts can see God
as He gives Himself to those who trust ...

in the hours of yesterday ...
He was there ...

in the times of today ...
He is here ...

in the moments of tomorrow ...
He will be there ...

for it is history ...

and it is His story ...

it is the present of His promise ...

it is the promise of His presence ...

He is the same ...
yesterday, today and tomorrow ...

He is God with us ...
He is Emmanuel ...

we have seen the images of God,
and they are the very things
for which that Bethlehem sky sang ...

His purpose is love ...
and His reason is you ...

Twenty-Three

<u>OUR EXAMPLE</u>

He became our example ...

He calls us to be His ambassadors ...

to be His voice ...
to be His eyes ...
to be His ears ...
to be His feet ...
to be His hands ...
to be His mind ...
to be His heart ...

to complete His work on this earth ...

may each dawn
bring us a renewed sense of commitment
to the task ...

trusting in the mission
and the message ...

believing
in ourselves ...
and in each other ...

bringing us a bit closer
to His purposes of
peace on earth ...
good will toward all ...

Twenty-Four

<u>THE SIMPLE PLAN</u>

We wanted a throne …
He gave us a manger …

we wanted a king …
He gave us a baby …

we wanted a ruler …
He gave us a carpenter …

we wanted it all …
and He gave us His all …

God gave His only begotten Son
so that all who believe in Him
should have eternal life …

it was
the grandest name …

giving the grandest gift …

wrapped in the grandest hope …

played out so simply …

a borrowed manger ...

a borrowed donkey ...

a borrowed tomb ...

with a message so simple ...

"come ...

follow ...

go" ...

it is easy to imagine the story
more complex, more difficult ...

but it is just so simply simple ...

a story majestically planned and presented ...

purposely and precisely ...

for you ...

Twenty-Five

A GREAT LIGHT

On a dark night in Bethlehem
our world was given a great Light ...

a radiant Light
that would guide God's people ...

and the Light that pierced the darkness
on that Bethlehem day
still promises us illumination
for all of our days ...

even in the darkness of Good Friday ...
Jesus, the Light of the World,
could not be extinguished ...

today He still shines brightly as our Savior ...

His Word still illuminates us ...

may we draw on that unfailing Light ...
may we let God's Light shine ...
to us ... through us ... beyond us ...
lifting His Light to all nations ...
and to all peoples ...

and may we continue to pass that Light on ...
and on ...
and on ...

Twenty-Six

<u>HE KNEW</u>

He knew in the stable ...
He knew in the Jerusalem parade ...
He knew in the garden ...
He knew at Calvary ...

He knew
we would doubt ...

He knew
we would stumble ...

but
it
did not matter ...

because His plan
included a holy blanket ...

a blanket of grace ...
a blanket of mercy ...
a blanket of forgiveness ...

a gift He planned before
we even knew to ask for it ...

a blanket for wrapping us in
when we have missed the mark ...
His holy blanket ...
because He knew ...

Twenty-Seven

FOUR GIFTS FOR YOU

Today, I pray for four gifts for you ...

and I pray that you might have these four gifts
not only on this day ...
but on all of your tomorrows ...

these four gifts do not take up much room
yet they could fill the earth ...

they cannot be touched
yet you can always carry them with you ...

these gifts can be felt
but not with your hands ...

they can be broken and shattered with neglect
but they are repairable if we take the time ...

they are not expensive
yet they are beyond priceless ...

your size does not matter
for these gifts fit everyone ...

the gifts must be fed, but interestingly enough
they will feed you more ...

while you feed these four gifts
they will quietly sustain you ...

their concept is simple
yet their meaning larger than life ...

these gifts carry no warranty
yet they have the Creator's guarantee ...

I pray not for your understanding of these gifts ...
simply for your experiencing of these gifts ...

may you take these four gifts
with you each day ...

may they shine most brightly
on your dark days ...

may you embrace these four gifts
and as you do ...
may you continually give them away ...
for the more they are used
the bigger they become ...

my friend,
the four gifts I pray for you are ...

His peace ...

His hope ...

His love ...

His joy ...

Twenty-Eight

<u>AFTER BETHLEHEM</u>

When it's time to pack away
the stars ...
the lights ...
the wreaths ...
the greens ...
may I keep out
part of
Christmas ...

the treasured part ...
the brilliance of Christ's birth ...
the belief of Mary ...
the trust of Joseph ...
the joy of the angels ...
the awe of the shepherds ...
the commitment of the wise men ...
the bold mentions of the Bethlehem baby ...
the prayers for peace on earth ...

yes ...
may I keep out
these
pieces
of
Christmas ...

Christmas does not need to be a season ...
Christmas can be a way of life ...

Twenty-Nine

<u>FROM THIS DAY ON</u>

From this day on
I want to be like Him ...

from this day on
I want to live like Him ...

from this day on
I want to listen like Him ...

from this day on
I want to speak like Him ...

from this day on
I want to walk with the unloved ...

from this day on
I want to hear the unheard ...

from this day on
I want to dine with the outcast ...

from this day on
I want to bind the wounds of the hurting ...

I want to honor the One
who gave us the living model for love ...
The One who took His first breaths
in that lowly manger bed ...
that is what I seek to do ... from this day on ...

Thirty

<u>THAT IS CHRISTMAS</u>

Every time
a kind word is spoken ...
that is Christmas ...

every time
a hand
reaches out to another ...
that is Christmas ...

every time
one sets aside self
to think of another ...
that is Christmas ...

every time
one sees the similarities
instead of the differences ...
that is Christmas ...

every time
one fights for good ...
that is Christmas ...

every time
someone shares love ...
the star of Bethlehem
shines ...

Thirty-One

<u>EACH MORNING</u>

Each morning
when you awake,
God's eyes are
already upon you ...

and each new day,
if you will let your heart listen ...

you will hear Him
whisper your name ...

inviting you to

"Awake ...

Arise ...

Come ...

FOLLOW ME" ...

Not THE END ...

just the beginning ...

To dear friends and editors ...
Janet Crow
Lisa Reese
Sherry Torbert

I give my loving thanks to you and for you ...

You are models of faith and friendship ...

You are precious gifts to me ...

love, Karen

For additional copies of
"Behold the Gift … the Blessings of Bethlehem"

Karen Anderson
Moments Publishing
5315B FM 1960 West #152
Houston, Texas 77069
281-989-3812
fax: 281-379-2002
www.MomentsPublishing.com
e-mail: info@MomentsPublishing.com